The Home Distiller's Workbook

Your guide to making moonshine, whiskey, vodka, rum, and so much more!

Jeff King

Published by FOI Publishing at
http://www.foipub.com.

Cover photo: Max Johnson
Cover model: Lavender Simone
Makeup: Miranda Barton

http://www.TheHomeDistiller.com

The information gathered in this book comes mostly from personal experience and from other publicly available sources. The purpose of this workbook is for entertainment and education only.

Please note that the distillation of alcohol without a license is against the law in the United States of America and many other countries. Please check your federal, state, and local laws prior to following any of the procedures outlined herein.

Better yet join us at www.LegalizeMoonshineNow.com and help us change these archaic laws!

Contents

Introduction

Man has been making alcohol since before recorded time. And in typically male fashion he decided that good was just not good enough, and he has been trying to make it better, and of course stronger, ever since. What we call distilling was really born in the twelfth century AD in southern Italy, and approximately five minutes later a local prince started taxing it. Or so the story goes. Needless to say, distillation and regulation seem to go hand in hand. It's sad that our government feels the need to keep such a tight leash on what is really a very simple and very easy process.

Whether it's just one tyrant a thousand miles away or a thousand tyrants just a few miles away, the government always seems to want the same thing: to keep us safe from ourselves. Oh, and to slap a tax on it while they're at it. Can't forget that.

Take one unjust law and add a commodity that everyone wants, and you get "moonshiners." Moonshiners are a breed apart. They risk life, limb, and even their very freedom, for the chance to make enough money to feed their families and carry them through to the next season. They have been hunted, hounded, outlawed, and persecuted. All for the public good. Or was it taxes? I get confused.

Today there's a new breed of outlaw. "Urban moonshiners," sometimes called "whiskey geeks," or as I prefer, just "shiners," take many of the same risks as traditional moonshiners. But the modern hobbyist isn't in it to make a profit. In fact, in many cases, it can be considerably cheaper to buy mass-produced booze right off the shelf.

But if they don't do it for the money, why take the risk? Some see it as a tantalizing hobby, others as a way to connect with our heritage, and still others as a way to stay independent and keep essential skills alive. I think most are simply trying to produce something better tasting than the mass-produced booze you find in your local store. The reasons are many, but ask any shiner and you'll probably get a nervous look, a wry smile, and a story that's as long as any about why he chose to bring this ancient profession back to life.

In this workbook you'll get a beginner's-level education in the world of distilling. First, I'll talk about how alcohol is produced, methods for distillation, and different ways to age and polish the product. I'll then discuss some of the more common types of spirits and even look at some recipes that home distillers are using to make their own. Lastly, I'll walk you step-by-step through the entire process of fermenting, distilling, and then aging your own spirits. Learning to distill is not a goal; it's a journey. And every journey has to start someplace. Yours is starting here. Mine, however, had a rougher start, far off in a land called…Kentucky!

My Kentucky Connection

It was the middle of my junior year in high school and my family had just moved from Omaha, Nebraska, to Cincinnati, Ohio. To many of you, Cincinnati may just sound like a typical Midwestern town. Trust me, it is not. Cincinnati is tucked down in the valleys and hills of the Ohio River, just on the southern border of the state. It is less typical Midwestern urban sprawl and more gateway to the South. Most of the friends that I found there had families and connections that went back across that river, sometimes all the way to the hills of Appalachia, as I was soon to discover.

My friends and I spent a good part of our summers back then across the river in Kentucky, cooling off at one swimming hole or another. One day we had gone to a decent-size creek to have a little party with some young ladies we had recently become acquainted with, when shortly thereafter a pickup truck came rolling up to our little shindig. The gentleman who got out of the truck was not in a pleasant frame of mind, and he hotly inquired as to who we were and why on god's green earth we had decided that it was a good idea to trespass on his land. Luckily for us, as chance would have it, he was not so distantly related to one of the members of our group. It was Kentucky, after all, and sooner or later you are going to run into either someone you are kin to or someone who knows someone you are kin to. So our friend apologized for us and generally tried to calm the landowner down. Just when it seemed that the whole thing was going to blow over, the man's eyes fell on me. At that time, in my late teens, I looked fairly straitlaced compared to most of my friends. Well, he eyed me up and down, and what came next was something that for some reason has always happened to me. He pointed at me and said, "He looks like a cop!" Yeah, I get that a lot. I was on the wrestling squad and played hockey and football as well, and my coaches, at least back then, made their players keep their hair high and tight. That combined with my good old-fashioned Midwestern manners always added up to the same thing. Whenever I dealt with anyone who might not appreciate those in law enforcement, I always seemed to get that "You look like a cop" response. Anyway, despite my friend's assurance that we went to high school together, and that he had known me forever, the landowner's paranoia was not so easily assuaged.

However, I had two of the finest social lubricants readily at hand. With one hand I offered him a cold, fresh-out-of-the-river can of Old Milwaukee, and with the other, a large if poorly rolled joint containing what at the time was simply the very top-of-the-line hydroponically grown hybrid of Skunk #1 and

Sense #5 that could be found in the Ohio River Valley. It was what we lovingly called "Christmas Tree." He actually grimaced at the beer but took the joint, sniffed it, and stopped. He eyed me and then he eyed my friends again. Turning back to me, he said, "Get in the truck and let's go for a drive." As he turned, I saw under his jacket the largest, shiniest revolver I'd ever seen, not that I had seen a lot of them. I decided quickly enough that it would be best to do as the man with the gun said. I figured a few puffs on that joint and I'd be his new best friend. It had worked for me before. I was praying that it would work again.

Well, he drove me down a long dirt road, and he didn't speak for about five of the longest minutes of my life. Then without a word he pulled my joint back out, handed it to me, and pointed to the cigarette lighter. So far, so good. This really was amazing stuff, even by Kentucky standards. A few puffs later and we were both well past anything close to straight and he had me going on and on about cars, girls, pot—you know, the important stuff to a seventeen-year-old. Suddenly we took a left turn where there was no road, just a break in the trees. The hills of Kentucky can be a beautiful sight on a glorious summer's day, but get down in one of those hollows, with the trees cutting off every inch of sunlight, and even midday can seem spookier than a Halloween night. Trust me on this. I could tell you about a Halloween night in the hills of Kentucky, a bag of weed, half a sheet of acid, and something about stolen horses. Not that I was there of course. I mean they shoot horse thieves, right? Let's just say that if I do a tour for this book I won't be stopping in Kentucky.

But back to our story. I'm now miles from my friends, stoned out of my mind, and riding through the woods of Kentucky in some armed lunatic's pickup. It's about this time that any sober fool would have started to panic. The next thing I know, he pulls the truck over next to a small shed in the middle of nowhere. He motions for me to get out and we go inside. At this point I'm expecting all sorts of horrible things. Scenes from horror movies are playing in my head to the musical accompaniment of dueling banjos. What I'm not expecting though is exactly what I see next: a still. There in the middle of this barn is a huge Rube Goldberg–like contraption. It was what you will come to refer to as a pot still. Seems that Senior here (if there was a Junior, I never did meet him) was a moonshiner, and he was so taken with the green stuff that I had shared with him that he wanted to show off some of the high-quality stuff that he made. Senior taught me about mash and corn, about how to get rid of the bad part of the run but keep the good part. He taught me also that moonshining is part of our country's heritage. About how this land was settled by people who relied on the skills required for distilling alcohol, and that it should never be forgotten. Over the next couple of years, I came down and helped him every so often. He would set up shop around July and then run through September. That was his season. He said that others started sooner and ran later but that they also got caught. I think I worked with him for three seasons or so before other things in life became too distracting and I had to move on.

Back to today. In the twenty-plus years since I met the moonshiner, I've been lucky to travel all over the world, and in doing so my knowledge of moonshining has brought about some pretty amazing experiences. It's like a club, and you can pretty much recognize the other members. In the Virgin Islands, I was at a local bar chatting with some of the regulars and I let it slip that I run a bit of shine back home. The next thing you know, we were in a car headed up into the hills to meet Victor, a.k.a. the "Rum Doctor." We spent the night drinking and swapping stories. Down in Mexico I met a fellow who barely spoke English but even so brought me home for dinner with his family so I could try his grandfather's tequila. In Northern California the mother of a friend insisted on showing me how she made grappa. And in Miami I met a guy who, in his quest to make the perfect vodka, takes the science of distilling to a level that NASA could learn from.

The nice thing about this hobby is that it isn't a perishable skill. You can try it now, put it down, and years later pick it back up. For me it's three or four times a year, for special events. I will brew up a batch or two for friends and family. If you think bringing out that expensive bottle of Scotch or vodka will liven up a party, then you need to see what happens when you bust out a mason jar of authentic Apple Pie Moonshine or some authentic Island-Style Dark Rum. Those will be parties that will not soon be forgotten.

In 2001 I gathered my notes, printed up some of the e-mails and forum posts that I had made over the years, and put together the first version of this book. That was ten years ago. In that time THDW went from an unknown book to a best seller in every category that it was listed in! Over the Christmas holiday of 2011, it even broke onto the list of the Amazon top thousand best-selling books. It was at this time I realized I was doing a disservice to my readers. I had not updated the book in almost a decade. Some of the information was out-of-date, and it was long overdue for a tune-up. I am now proud to bring you this new and improved 3rd edition.

Thank you all for being so patient.
Jeff King

A Beginner's Guide to Distilling

There are a lot of misconceptions about what distilling is. Before we get too deep, I want to take a moment to address a couple of key issues.

- Distillation is the process of separating one liquid from another.
- Distilling is NOT a means for creating alcohol. Fermenting the mash, or what traditionalists call beer, is the process where alcohol is created.
- Fermenting is the process of allowing yeast, in a controlled environment, to consume the sugars from your mash and turn them into alcohol.
- Ethanol (alcohol) is made during the fermentation of sugars, grains, and/or fruits. Methanol is a poisonous alcohol made from wood-based products.
- The process of distilling alcohol includes three stages: fermenting, distilling, and finally aging.

Fermenting—Wikipedia defines ethanol fermentation as "a biological process in which sugars such as glucose, fructose, and sucrose are converted into cellular energy and thereby produce ethanol and carbon dioxide as metabolic waste products." In other words, the little yeast monsters eat all the sugar in your mash and give off alcohol and CO_2 as a by-product.

It really is a simple process. To ferment your own mash, you will need four items: Sugar, Yeast, Nutrients and lastly Water.

Sugar—It can be sugar straight out of a bag or from any food that has high natural sugar content, whether a grain or fruit, which are the most common sources of sugar, or even other products like sugarcane, beets, or potatoes

If you are trying to get your sugars from grains you will need to include an extra step, malting. The old-school way to "malt" your grains is to simply let them go to seed. Let them sprout to about a one-quarter inch and then dry them. Those sprouts contain amino acids that help break down the starches in the grain and convert them into sugar for the yeast. Another option is to add brewer's malt to the mash. This is something that, back in the day, could be found in any grocery store but can be a bit trickier to find these days. Luckily the Internet can still save the day.

Yeast – This is the workhorse of the process. Yeast is a fungus that will consume sugar and leave behind CO_2 and ethanol. The problem is that too much ethanol is actually toxic to the yeast. Once the percentage of ethanol gets above 10% or so it starts killing most strains of yeast. This is why your average mash will only yield about 10% alcohol by volume (ABV). The good news is that there are now strains of fast-acting yeast, or "turbo yeast," that can tolerate higher levels of ethanol, up to 20% and maybe even higher. With these "distiller yeasts," you can almost double your production.

Nutrients – If you want your yeast to work as hard as it can they will need more then just sugar, the yeast needs nutrients as well. This is something that they get from all the grains and fruits in your mash and really isn't an issue unless you are doing a pure sugar mash. You can get around that by adding DME (Dried Malt Extract) to your starter (more on "starters" later). Or you can use a pre packaged Turbo Yeast. Most turbos are premixed with all the nutrients that the yeast will ever need.

Water—The last but still vital ingredient. You need good, clean water for a quality drink. Remember, in the end, 50% or so of your drink will be water. Bottled water works fine, although some prefer distilled and others fresh spring water for the minerals and flavors that it brings. If you are using fresh spring water, please make sure to boil and filter it first. There can be nasty bugs living in your pure mountain fresh water.

The basic process for creating a mash is to bring your water up to a boil, add in your ingredients of choice. Cook it until you have extracted all the sugars, and then cool the whole thing to just above room temperature, about 70°F.

Now it's time to pitch the yeast. Pitching is simply the act of adding your yeast to the mash. There are two ways in which to purchase yeast, dry and liquid. For dry yeast you can pour it strait into your fermenter. Or you can make a starter. Starters are good way to get your yeast up and working, also they are pretty much required when using a liquid yeast.

FUN FACT – When you make bread and let it rise, it's the CO_2 from the yeast that does the lifting! Not only that, but there is alcohol in there as well. Sadly, it quickly evaporates.

If you are making a mash that is five gallons or greater in volume you really should consider making a starter. A starter will allow the yeast to grow so that you will have enough yeast to do the work that is needed and it will also let you know that your yeast is active and healthy. Just consider spending the hours it takes to brew something like this up, then putting in a fermenter and waiting a week only to find out that your yeast was dead. It can and does happen. Starters should be made no less then 20 minutes before they are needed. Personally I make mine on Monday or Tuesday for the brewing I do on Saturday.

So here is what you need to do to make a yeast starter:

- Sterilize everything you will use. You can do this with a typical bleach and water solution but I highly recommend one of the brewing specific products like Sani-Star. Just follow the instructions on the back.
- In a saucepan bring a 2.5 cups of water to a boil.
- Reduce heat and add ½ cup of dry malt extract.
- Mix thoroughly.
- Bring to a light boil for ten minutes.
- Remove from heat and allow to cool to 70F or thereabouts..
- Pour into a sterilized bowl or bottle, I use Erlenmeyer flasks for that mad scientist feel.
- Cover and shake bottle well to oxygenate the liquid.
- Add the contents of the yeast container.
- Cover and shake bottle well, again.
- Loosen cover so that it is not airtight, and leave bottle in a room where it will not get direct sunlight but will stay in the 75°F to 80°F range.

- It is best to place the bottle on a stir plate, but if you don't have one (and really, who does?) just give it a light circular stir every time you walk by.
- Shake the whole bottle just before pouring into your mash.

PRO TIP: Stir plates rock. They are normally something you only find in a lab and they cost upwards of $100. Or you can head over to http://stirstarters.com/. There you can find directions on how to make one for less then $20 or you can buy a prebuilt model from them for $45 and it comes with the stir bar and holder magnet. They sell those cool flasks too.

To pitch the yeast, gently pour it into your mash. Gently shake the container to mix the yeast in. Now you should cork it and add your air lock. The air lock is a device half-filled with water that will allow the CO_2 to escape without allowing oxygen in. Why? Because what is going on down there is that the yeast is happily eating all your sugar and trying to use all that energy to make new yeast, but it needs oxygen to do that. When we deprive it of oxygen it becomes anaerobic and stops trying to reproduce. Instead it releases its built-up energy as CO_2 and…ALCOHOL!

Now take your container and put it someplace dark and cool, right around 70°F. If your mash gets too cold the yeast will go dormant, zzzzzzzzzzzz. Sleepy yeast produces no alcohol. Alternatively, if the mash gets too warm, the yeast will die.

The catch here is that as the yeast produces alcohol two things will happen. The first is a chemical reaction, and as with many reactions of this type, it gives off heat, so as the yeast works your mash will warm up. Second, as the level of alcohol increases the temperature needed to kill off the yeast gets steadily lower.

Now, depending on the percentage of alcohol and the type of yeast you are using, the number can vary, but the general rule of thumb you need to know for now is to keep your fermenter at 75°F. At this temperature your typical five-gallon mash will only take three days to ferment, whereas at 60°F it could take two weeks to produce and at 85°F or so most yeast will start to die.

Some of you are thinking, but what if I'm at 83°F, won't that be faster? Yes it will be, but not that much faster, and at that high a temperature the yeast will make more of some of the other by-products, the nasty stuff like congeners. We will talk more about that later, but for now, set your cruise control to 75°F. If your mash gets too cold, you can put it in a warm room and cover it with a blanket to keep the heat in. Or just hold it close, and warm it with your love. If it gets too hot, move it to a cooler room, or point a small portable fan at it.

Pro Tip—When your mash is ready, instead of just pouring it out, use a siphon tube to extract the clean liquid off of the top while leaving the yeast and other particles on the bottom undisturbed. This will make it easier to distill.

Distilling—Now the fun begins. Distilling is an art and a science all rolled into one. Let us discuss the science first.

Wikipedia tells us that distillation is "a method of separating mixtures based on differences in volatility of components in a boiling liquid mixture" and that it "is a unit operation, or a physical separation process, and not a chemical reaction."

Um, yeah. OK, now in English. Distilling alcohol is the process of heating up the mash to the point where the alcohol turns into a vapor, which luckily for us is just before water turns into a vapor.

You see, ethanol boils at 173°F but water doesn't boil till it gets up to 212°F. This means that if you can keep what I call the break-over point above 173°F but below 212°F, then the alcohol in the mixture will boil, turn into a vapor, and rise up into the still to then be cooled and collected while the water and other contaminants stay in the pot! It really is just that simple.

Mastering the art of distilling involves more then just knowing boiling points and how to read a thermometer. Its about learning all the nuances and quirks of your still and figuring out just how to run it.

Some stills heat up very quickly and cool off quickly, while those that heat up slowly also cool at a slower rate and thus retain heat better. Think of using a still like operating the gas and brake pedals of your car. You need to stick to that speed limit. And while a quick throttle response may sound good at first, that also means that it's easy to overheat your mash. But the same goes for the slower still. When it starts to get too hot, it can be harder to back the temperature down.

It's also important to know what parts of your still get hot and how fast they respond to adjustments in temperature. I mentioned a term before, the break-over point. Think of it as the point of no return. It's the point in a still's heating cycle where the steam has risen as far as it's going to go and it is now getting cooler and cannot get back into the boiling chamber. So the only other way out is down through the condenser and into the collector. It's important to figure out where this spot is and to monitor the temperature there as well. It's only when you know all the characteristics of your still that you will be able to get the best performance out of it.

To run your still, follow these steps:

- Strain your mash through a cheese cloth or similar fine-grade strainer.
- Pour your mash into the boiling chamber of the still. Leave enough room for expansion due to foam and such. I usually fill it about two-thirds to three-fourths full.
- Close up your still, making sure there are no leaks where vapor may escape and ignite!
- Turn on your fan to cool your condenser or turn on the pump for the water jacket.
- Make sure your space is well ventilated. Turn on exhaust fans as needed.
- Go to the bathroom now, as once you turn on your heat you are here for the duration. You never leave a working still unattended.
- Turn on the heat and sit back and watch.
- Monitor your still and your temperatures. Take notes.

- Note when the boiling chamber reaches 148.5°F as this is when poisonous methanol starts to boil.
- Make sure the collector is in place.
- Carefully manage the temperature as it approaches 173°F. You want to make sure that you are very, very slowly raising the temperature of your still. This will allow all the bad stuff to gather at the top of your still so it can all get collected in one pass.
- Collect your foreshots (the nasty stuff) and toss them. Do not mess with this stuff. They don't just taste bad, they are poisonous!
- Your foreshots will equal approximately a quarter of a percent, or 0.25 percent of your total mash, but I say be ruthless and double that to half of a percent, or 0.5 percent. You should, however, calculate this amount based on what you put in the still on each run. So, if you put a gallon of mash into your still, then the first 0.639 fluid ounces should get tossed. But Red's Rule is round up for safety! Just toss that whole first ounce. BE RUTHLESS, I SAY! There is plenty more where that came from so don't fret about drops and drabs.
- Next we get to the heads. The heads are the first part of the real ethanol. The bad news is that they also contain some other stuff like the congeners I

mentioned. You will want to collect these in a separate container and set them aside.

- How can you tell when you are past the heads? Practice, my good man! But honestly it's the smell. The heads will have a smell to them that is specific to the kind of mash you made. Collect some of the drops coming out onto your finger or the back of a spoon and smell them. Once you are past the heads, the smell will start to disappear.

- Now just sit back and collect all that alcohol that we made in the fermenter. One six-gallon bucket of mash, even at only 10 percent ABV, should get you the equivalent of three 750 mL bottles of fine drinking hooch!

- Last we come to the tails. When your still starts getting close to 200°F, say 198°F or so, you are most likely done. Your alcohol has been extracted and you are at the tails.

- The tails can be used to add flavor to your run. If you are running a whiskey or some other strong-flavored drink, then go ahead and run it till it gets up closer to 200°F. But don't go too far or your flavor will be off.

- One of the signs that you are into the tails is the presence of fusel oils. The trick that was taught to me for identifying these is to dip your finger into the output and then rub your fingers together. Does it feel slick, like very lightweight oil? Also, you can take your collector and look at the surface. Is it multicolored like a rainbow? Yep, that's the fusel oils. Don't add this to your drink, but do save it.

- I figure out ahead of time how much I should get from my still and then I divide that into small units and collect them separately. That way I can keep the heart of the run separate and then mix back in the other components to taste!

- Also I run the rest of my still, tails and all, until only water is coming out and then shut it down there. I take what is left over from the heads and the tails, the stuff I decide not to use, and I add that to the next batch that I'm going to run. This serves a few purposes. It helps to ensure a continuity of flavor between batches, and it reduces the amount of energy it will take to cook up the next batch while also helping increase its stability.

Aging—This is the final phase of the process. I'll be honest here and say that this step is entirely optional. There is nothing that says that you must do anything to age or polish your spirits. Just don't expect me to try them. I've drank my share of pure shine and I'm old enough now to want something a bit more refined.

Aging/polishing is the process of filtering or exposing the spirits to other elements that help remove the things that give the drink a hard edge in order to make it more palatable. Also this is the stage where much of the flavor is generated. This can be as simple as running the drink through an activated carbon filter, much like you would find in a Brita water pitcher. Or it can be as complex as filtering, casking, and then even infusing the drink with fruits or nuts. I love a good bourbon that has been infused with cherries. OK, so the bourbon is fine, but it's the cherries that are the real treat. They turn into little hundred-proof bourbon bombs!

Part of the aging step is the cutting of your spirits. If you have 85 percent ABV, you are going to want to cut that down to 50 or maybe even 40 percent. I suggest sticking with whatever type of water you used in your wash. If you used spring water for a whiskey, then continue to use that. For vodka, you will probably want 100 percent pure distilled water. Feeling bold? Use fruit juices or other liquids. Remember, whatever you add is going to end up being 50 percent or greater of the final product. So don't go through all the effort to get to this point only to get cheap on your cutting agent. You can only get out of this what you put into it.

Also, if you are aging in wooden barrels, there will be some evaporation. This is normal and is called the angels' share.

Concepts and Practices

This is the point where things can really get confusing. Every person that you will talk to on this subject has a different method of getting to what is essentially the same end product. And what's worse is that there really isn't any best way of doing it. The reason for this is because it's really an issue of preference. Distilling, just like cooking, comes down to your personal tastes.

Personally, I'm a bourbon drinker. This means that I almost always use a pot still and stick to a grain mash. A pot still is the most basic of the "true" stills. It usually requires multiple runs or the use of an attachment called a thumper and it will carry over a good amount of the flavor from the original beer or mash. A good friend of mine will only touch vodka, and that's her loss if you ask me, but she knows what she likes. She uses a potato-and-sugar mash and runs it through a good-size still called a column still. This strips the alcohol in one pass. It would normally take multiple runs with a pot still to get that level of purity.

Before we go any further, let's take a moment to discuss some of the most common distilling concepts and still designs.

Sour Mash—You will see a lot of whiskeys advertised as "sour mash." This just means that some of the mash from a previous fermentation that still has yeast in it has been pulled back and added to the new mash. This does a couple of things. It helps to stabilize the acids and jump-start the yeast in the new mash, and it also helps to keep the flavor consistent from one run to the next.

Back Set—A back set is a portion of a previous run of sprits added to the finished product of the next run. Say you take 20 percent of whatever you make and hold it back. Then when you distill your next batch, you pour that in there, mix it around, and then take out another 20 percent at the end of the run. And repeat this with every run. Why? Continuity of flavor.

Steam Distilling—The most common method of distilling is by heating the mash to the point where the alcohol becomes a gas but not so hot that the water and other liquids vaporize as well.

The Break-Over Point—With steam distilling, what you are essentially trying to do is very gently push the alcohol vapor up a hill. At the top of that hill you want to have it balanced just right so that only a slight nudge will carry it over to the other side. This top of the hill is your break-over point. Here, the still is just hot enough that the alcohol vapor will crest over the apex of the lyne arm to continue to the condenser for collection. All the other stuff, water and other ingredients, will not have enough energy or heat to make it to the top and will instead collect on the various plates, or surfaces in the still, and reflux back into your boiling chamber. Once you have a firm grasp of this concept, everything else will probably seem like common sense to you. I've placed a red lightning bolt in each of the still illustrations that follow, to indicate the break-over point on the still. Remember that every still is different, but once you have determined the break-over point on your still you will be able to dial in the exact taste you want.

Plates —This is one of the more advanced concepts and one you really don't even need to concern yourself with, at least not to start with. But I include it here for those of you that are looking for a little something extra. That being said, a plate is any surface in a still where the vapor reaches a condensation point and flows back into the boiling chamber. This is called reflux. The more plates that alcohol vapor touches, the more stripped down it becomes. Thus the more reflux a still has, the purer the end product. In the case of most pot stills, there are two plates, the top of the boiling chamber and the lyne arm.

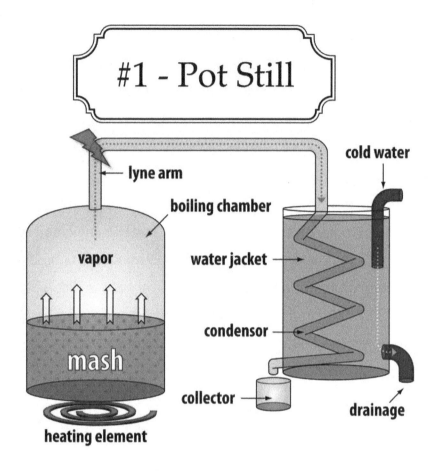

#1 - Pot Still

lyne arm

boiling chamber

cold water

vapor

water jacket

condensor

mash

collector

drainage

heating element

Pot Still (figure 1) —The pot still is probably the original of the steam-based stills. It can be very basic in design, requiring only three components: a boiling chamber, a lyne arm, and a condenser. The mash is heated in the boiling chamber. As it turns to steam, it rises to the top of the boiling chamber and then along the lyne arm to the condenser. The condenser is cooled, either by air or cold water. The steam hits the cooled metal of the condenser and turns to liquid, where it runs down and drips into your collector. Pot stills come in many variations. Is the top of your still conical, rounded, or flat? Conical will allow the steam to escape easier, reduce reflux, and increase flavor. A flat surface will present more of a barrier and produce more contact, increase reflux, and reduce flavor. A rounded still top will give you something in between.

Another consideration in controlling the output of the still is the tilt of the lyne arm. As you can see in figure 2, the lyne arm can be adjusted to control inversely for either purity of the alcohol vapor or for flavor. Say your boiling chamber has a flat top and you want more flavor. Change your lyne arm to tilt down and you should recover some flavor. I'd start with something in the middle range and then adjust to taste.

#2 - Lyne Arm

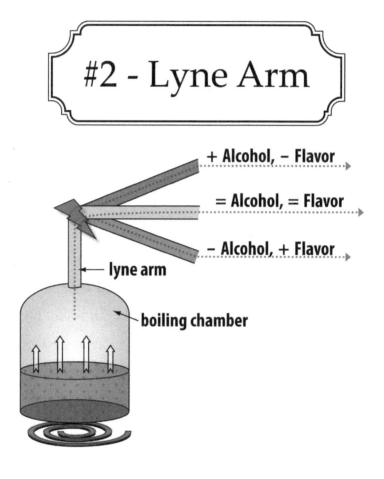

+ Alcohol, – Flavor

= Alcohol, = Flavor

– Alcohol, + Flavor

lyne arm

boiling chamber

The basic idea of the lyne arm is that reflux is equal to surface contact. The greater the surface, the more the vapor will collect, with only the purest alcohol vapor making it to the condenser—the caveat being that pure alcohol has little taste. Pot stills are good for whiskey, tequila, and other flavorful liquors. The normal yield from a pot still is around 40 percent ABV. To get your batch up to drinkable levels, 80 to 90 percent, you have to do one of two things: (1) run whatever you collect through your still a second time, or (2) use a thumper (figure 3). For your first several runs, I suggest you stick with the basics and just run it a second time. Once you have that mastered, you can try adding a thumper.

What is a thumper? Well, the truth is that there are two other components that are often incorporated into a pot still: a thumper box and a slobber box (figure 3).

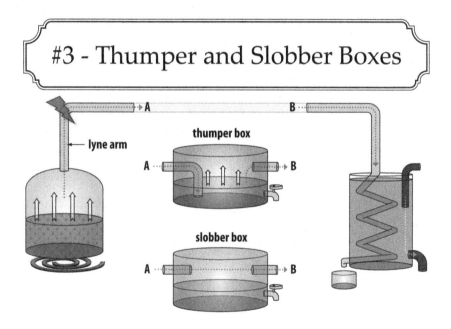

#3 - Thumper and Slobber Boxes

With a thumper the steam is forced below the surface of a liquid (usually some alcohol left over from a previous run). As the vapor bubbles up through this liquid, any foam or other solids are filtered out. This steam in turn heats the contents of the thumper. Soon the liquid will reach the point where it starts to vaporize yet again. The vapor continues on to the condenser, while some is returned to a liquid state and collects in the thumper. In essence you are distilling twice with just one run! The key here is that you must fill your thumper with a liquid that contains a sufficient amount of alcohol. Usually I just run my still with the thumper empty. Then, once I get enough liquid to fill the thumper, I back down the temperature a bit to slow down the still, swap out my collector, and quickly pour the contents into the thumper. *Voilà!*

A slobber box looks a lot like a thumper except that the line coming in does not go below the lid of the box. The slobber box is used to collect foam and other solids that may have boiled over into the lyne arm. The slobber box collects these and allows the vapor to continue on to the condenser. Think of it as a filter.

Pro Tip —To be honest, a well-run still shouldn't need a slobber box. But whether you are using a thumper or a slobber box, be sure to include a drainage valve so that you can regulate the fluid level during the run.

#4 - Reflux Still

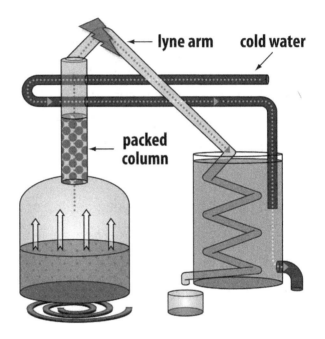

Reflux Still (figure 4) — A popular choice among hobbyists, this still provides the best of both worlds. Instead of a regular tube leading to the lyne arm, the reflux still has a larger column, packed with an inert material. This material can be anything from stones to marbles but Raschig rings (small ceramic rings) are most commonly used.

Above this part of the column, near the top, two cooling tubes pass through. These tubes are on the same system as the water that feeds into the water jacket for the condenser. The cooling tubes add another reflux element and help this still produce an end product with higher alcohol content.

Because of the added reflux elements, most of the alcohol vapor will condense on one of these plates and drip back into the boiling chamber. This means that the vapor that does reach the condenser will be much higher in alcohol content than that from a pot still.

So a reflux still is good for making neutral spirits, such as vodka, gin, and rum. The real advantage is that you can "detune" the still by removing the packing material. With the packing material removed and the cooling tubes bypassed, it will operate just like a traditional pot still.

Fractional/Column Still —This is the big brother of the reflux still. It has a taller column, often insulated, and can use any number of condensers. For the most part, only serious hobbyists will use a still of this type due to its complexity. Also, all mash passed through it will be completely stripped of any flavor and you will only get straight alcohol in return. Since sugar is usually cheaper than other fermenting ingredients, I recommend that you run only sugar-based mashes through this type of still. Stills of this type are used for making vodka or for alcohols that will be flavored. It is also the preferred still for ethyl alcohol fuel production.

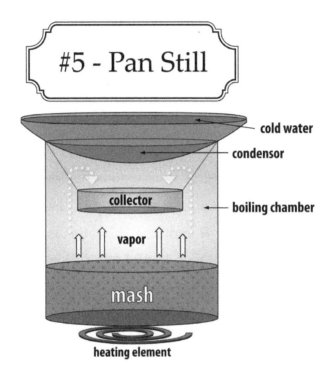

Pots Still (figure 5) —This is the favorite of the casual kitchen distiller. With as little as three pans, which you probably already have in your kitchen, you can make great brandies and schnapps. Place the mash, or wine as it's sometimes called, boiling chamber, usually a stock pot and heat slowly until you start to see steam. At this point place the collector pan so that it hangs beneath the condenser (I like to use a wok) but well above the mash in the boiling chamber. Now fill the condenser with chilled water or ice. As the steam rises, it will condense on the underside of the cooled pan and drip back into the collector pan. The downside of this technique is that it is very hard to monitor. Doing cuts and such are very difficult, controlling the temperature can be a bit of a chore, and a good bit of the steam is lost due to this being an open system.

Freeze Distillation — Wherever man goes he finds a way to make alcohol. And then some numbnut says, "Hey, I bet we can make that stronger!" Rumor has it that this is how the Inuits make their booze. The principle behind it is so easy it's scary. Simply put, water freezes before alcohol. To do this you will need a large bowl and a fine strainer. That's it. Take your mash and strain out all solids. Pour into a bowl and place in your freezer. After it is frozen solid, take it out and place the bowl upside down in the strainer. Put another bowl underneath the strainer. Stop when about half the ice has melted or starts to look clear. This will basically double the alcohol content in the output that you collect. This is an easy way to bump up your mash from the usual 10 percent ABV to almost 20 percent.

Pro Tip—Place a beer or even a soda in your freezer. Best to pour it in a glass first! Let it freeze mostly solid. Take it out and break up the ice. Pour through a strainer into another glass and taste. Strong isn't it. And you'll notice that the ice is mostly clear. The slower the freezing process, the purer the resulting drink. Try it with wine and other lower-alcohol-content drinks. Two Buck Chuck is a good candidate for this.

Setting Up Your First Still

The Tea Pot Still—Using the simple old-fashioned whistling tea pot is a great way to make a small but easy-to-use still. And did I mention cheap. An older Italian guy showed me how to do this. Proof, once again, that man will find a way to get his drink on! Did I mention that he made the most amazing Limoncello?

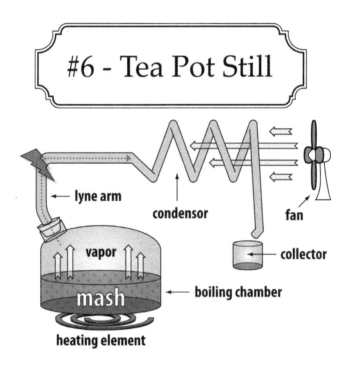

#6 - Tea Pot Still

lyne arm

condensor

fan

vapor

collector

mash

boiling chamber

heating element

OK, recruits, here is your shopping list:

- Tea pot. The larger the better. I usually use a 2½-quart model. There are two basic types of tea pots. The old-fashioned style, where the only opening is in the spout, and the type that also has a lid. The old-fashioned style is the easiest to use but hardest to clean. If you use one with a lid, make sure that it is a very simple lid made of metal and doesn't have any sort of plastic on it. You will need to seal any openings. (See the next "Pro Tip)

- Copper tubing.
- Cooking thermometer or digital thermometer. I even like to use those infrared ones with the laser. Yes, I have a gadget problem.
- Cork or rubber stoppers. You can find these at some kitchen stores, or better yet, your local wine and beer making shop. And, as always, online.
- A two-cup measuring glass.
- Twine.
- Small fan.
- Optional: a tube bender. The cheap, spring variety will do.
- Optional: a tube cutter. Get the cheap, four-dollar one. You are only going to use it a couple of times, so no need to waste the money.
- Optional: compression fittings, but only if you are feeling really frisky. Make sure they say "Lead Free" on them!

There are three things you need to consider when setting up your still: ventilation, a heat source, and cooling your condenser. Everyone knows that the first rule when handling a gun is to always treat it like it's loaded. My first rule of running a still is to assume that at some point your still WILL give off alcohol vapors. If they hit an ignition source, like say the burner on your stove, you are going to have a problem. Don't let this happen. The key to this is ventilation, so open the window and turn on your vent/fan. I'm probably overstating the danger here. In all my years of doing home distilling, I've never once heard of anyone setting their kitchen on fire, much less injuring themselves. Can the same be said of people deep-frying turkeys? Just the same, let's all be safe, not sorry.

How to heat your pot? Electrical heat, while slower, is the safest. I wouldn't rule out the purchase of a single-burner hot plate. They only cost around fifteen dollars. But I'm a lover of gas and I won't tell you not to use it. Gas gives instant heat and allows better precision for controlling your temperature, but the choice is yours.

Lastly, you'll need a way to cool down the condenser. Most hobbyists use a water-cooled condenser (figure 7), but to start with we will use a basic air-cooled coil (figure 6). With this setup I can cook in the comfort of my kitchen. I set my still on my stove, a few feet from my sink. The lyne arm goes up two feet and then makes a ninety-degree angle back down to my condenser. My condenser is simply coiled tubing that sits next to my sink and is cooled by a small electric fan. The last part of the tubing from my condenser goes down into my sink where I use my measuring glass as my collector. This still is the very epitome of KISS (Keep It Simple, Schmuck). I know that after reading all this material you will be all excited and thinking about how you are going to make the biggest still and run it through a thumper and into a water-jacketed condenser (figure 7) and get 180 proof alcohol on your first run. STOP! Learn to walk before you run. Trust me, even the pros started off learning the basics. Learn the basics well and then you will know more than the guy who started up with some fancy Internet-purchased fractional still.

#7 - Water Jackets

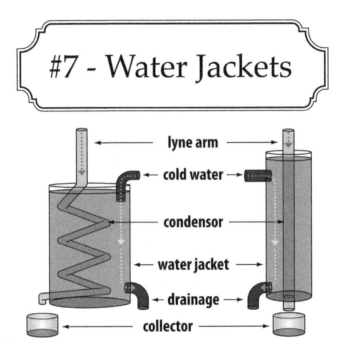

So to make your tea pot still…

- Place your still where you are going to cook.
- Use thread to mock up the lyne arm and condenser placement.
- Measure the thread, this will tell you how much tubing you need. Always buy a little more than you need.
- Using something hard and round, like say a wine bottle or a tube bender, gently bend the tube to the shape you need. Here is where the compression fittings come into place. If you don't want one big piece of copper, then cut it into two smaller sections that are easier to clean and handle. These can then be joined with the

compression fittings. All you need is an adjustable wrench. It's very easy. It's also something that can be done later, so I would suggest that for now you just stick with a single piece of tubing.

- Now put your tea kettle in place. Put the stopper on the end of the lyne arm and push it into the mouth of the kettle.

- Now you need to support the lyne arm and condenser. There are a couple of different ways to do this and I'm sure you can figure out what will work best for you. In my kitchen I simply use that same twine and tie it to my condenser. I then run it up and over the door of my kitchen cabinet and tape it to the back of the door. Remember, keeping things simple really is the best way to accomplish even the most difficult tasks.

Depending on how tight your stopper is, you may have to work with it to get it completely sealed. To test the system, just boil some water in it and look for any leaks. A little soapy water applied to a questionable area will produce bubbles if there is a leak.

Pro Tip—An old trick to seal up any leaks and make sure you have an air tight seal is to make up a batch of flour and water or what we like to call Moonshiner's Biscuits.

- Put some flour in a bowl.
- Add water and mix till it is doughy/pasty.
- Liberally smear this anywhere there is a connection or leak you want to make air tight. Think of it like caulk.
- As the still comes up to heat, the dough will bake right onto the still. Moonshiner's Biscuits.

Pro Tip II—Don't eat 'em. They taste like crap. My dog, however, loves 'em. He is a bit touched though if you know what I mean.

How easy was that? I also need to point out that the height and degree of angle of your lyne arm are up to you. The reason mine goes straight up two feet is that when I'm distilling more neutral spirits such as vodka or gin I will put a fan to blow on that section to cool it down, kind of the way a reflux still would work. If it gets too cold, I just wrap it in some foil-wrap insulation to keep in the heat.

Distilling and Fermenting Equipment

Just as with any hobby, there is a ton of optional equipment that you might need. OK, so some of it not so optional. You can buy most of this stuff piecemeal at either a grocery store or even the hardware store. Some of the more special items are a little harder to find though. You can check out my Amazon.com store here, www.MoonshiningSupplies.com I've put together a collection of supplies to help get you started. You can find most everything you will need there but if you can't find it, just e-mail us and we will help you find it.

Back to our shopping list. Here are some other components that you will need at some point:

- large metal spoons for stirring
- large wire strainers
- small, medium, and large plastic funnels
- oven mitts
- mixing bowl
- 2-cup glass measuring cup
- electric fan(s)
- ziplock freezer bags
- vapor locks
- wort chiller (very optional, if you don't know what this is don't bother)
- and more!

Thermometer—You will need at least two thermometers. One for the fermenting and one for the still. The thermometer on the fermenter doesn't need to be too accurate as it's only a guideline. It needs to show the range between 50°F and 100°F. I use the stick-on-strip type like you would use in an aquarium. You will need this to make sure that the fermenter stays in the appropriate temperature range. (As I noted earlier, too hot and the yeast will die, not hot enough and the yeast will become dormant, and no one likes sleepy yeast.) I've found that 75°F is a pretty good temperature for most yeast but as always I defer to the instructions on your yeast packet.

For the second thermometer, you will need a good-quality cooking one. It needs to read up to 225°F and should be fairly accurate. You will need to be able to tell when you are at 173°F.

Pro Tip—I also use a touchless, infrared, laser-guided thermometer. These used to be big bucks but now can be had for under fifty dollars. I use this for spot checks on the burner, the lyne arm, the condenser, for checking the kids' rooms at night, for testing the coals on the BBQ, to torment the cat, and so much more.

Hydrometer— (Optional) Eventually you will want one of these so you can make accurate adjustments and keep detailed notes. You will need two of these, one for the mash and one for your end product (sometimes called an Alcoholmeter). The first one, for the wash, is the regular hydrometer used by beer makers. The second is for the hard alcohol. It may be harder to find. It is usually lighter and more accurate. This one will tell you what percentage of alcohol you have distilled—and thus the proof—and by this you can get a good gauge of how your still is working.

Pro Tip—Hydrometers are sensitive to temperature. Make sure you use this tool at the temperature specified by the manufacturer.

Fermenter—This is nothing more than a big container that you put your mash in and make the alcohol with. About anything will do, but above all else the fermenter has to be able to be easily cleaned and sterilized. It should have a good, airtight lid on it and a hole for an air lock. The air lock is usually about five dollars, and is an odd-shaped bit of plumbing that holds some water in it: outgoing gases can bubble out through the liquid, but nothing can find its way in. A simple alternative is to just run a tube from the top of the fermenter, ending in a jar half-filled with water. Why the air lock? Once the yeast is off and running, you don't want there to be any oxygen in the system, or else the yeast will forget about making alcohol, and just make more yeast. So don't have it breezy. But you don't want it airtight, or else the carbon dioxide (CO_2) made by the yeast will build up in pressure and blow the lid off. It's also nice if you are doing a big batch to have a tap near the base of the fermenter so that you can easily run off the wash once it has finished fermenting.

If you are doing small runs, I recommend going and buying a gallon of that fancy apple cider that comes in that big glass jug. For bigger stuff we sell ten-gallon food-grade buckets. They have an airtight snap on the lid with a hole cut out for your bubbler.

Pro Tip—A couple of things that I use to speed up the process are an electric juicer and a food processor. Remember that what we are really after is the sugar; most of the sugar is in the juice. Also by running your materials through a food processor you increase the surface area and allow it to interact more with the wash. But don't go overboard. We are just trying to crack the grains. Just make the chunks a little smaller, don't pulverize them. If you want to get all fancy you can invest in a grain mill.

Facts, Myths, and Things You Need to Know

The Law—The first thing you need to know is this. In most countries OPERATING A STILL WITHOUT PROPER LICENSING/PERMITS IS ILLEGAL. As such I'm operating under one of three assumptions:

- That you either live in one of the civilized countries, such as New Zealand, where they have shown that allowing people to operate their own stills has not proved any more of a hazard to the general public than allowing the use of microwave ovens.

- That you have those said permits. Which, by the by, I've looked into (in the USA), and, no, you are not going to get one. The laws are designed from the get-go to keep Joe Average out of the business and to keep Big Liquor safe from the little guys. It would seem that they feel they have much to fear. Stuff like competition and innovation. You know, American values, but I digress.

- Or that you are looking at this book for entertainment and/or educational purposes, perhaps to better educate yourself for when you write those e-mails to your congressperson and senator to tell them that they had better start setting some things straight or start looking for new jobs.

Fire—The next-greatest risk to distillers is that of fire. You're producing a liquid whose flammability is on par with that of gasoline. On top of that, you are doing so around heating elements (or even gas flames). What kind of idiot are you? Give up on this and just go by a bottle.

Make sure that there is no way you can build up pressure inside your still—by blocking the outlet piping (say, by accidentally crimping it?).

Pro Tip—Distilling is a low- to no-pressure system. This is why I advise not using pressure cookers or anything else that locks down too tight. If something does go wrong and your still does pressurize, then a loosely connected top that will just pop off is a nice and easy safety mechanism.

Make sure your equipment is in good condition when you use it, that it's clean (you don't want the packing material clogging up and blocking), and that there are no leaks. Don't bury the outlet tube under the surface of the liquid level in the collector; rather, have it dripping into it openly. If you are using gas, keep the collection jar a good distance from the source. Don't set up your collection jars so that they are easily knocked over, and cap them when not in use. Keep your area well ventilated, never leave the still unattended, and keep a fire extinguisher close.

Blindness—If you tell people that you make your own moonshine, someone will say, "You know you can go blind from that stuff." It's like a law or something. And this is often a big fear for many new distillers. This disinformation was started by the US government as a way to try and keep people from buying moonshine during prohibition. Yet as with any good lie there is some truth behind it. Methanol is a toxin that can cause blindness by affecting the optic nerve. Drink a bunch of methanol and you can go blind or even die. But we are making "ethanol" here, or at least you had better be. As long as you are starting with a mash made from fruits, sugars, and grains, you will only get the smallest bit of methanol in your mash and it can be easily discarded with the foreshots collected at the beginning of your run.

Heads or Tails—To get a really clean distinction between the foreshots and the rest of the alcohol, slowly increase the temperature at the beginning of your run so that you are taking off this first 5 percent at a very slow rate, say, one drop per second. This will make it much easier to tell once all the nasty bits are gone.

How dangerous are these "fusel oils"? Well, they can do a lot more than just give you a headache, but that is why I always say that you should be ruthless about tossing the first heads. It's always better to err on the side of caution than to risk making someone sick or even just ruining your whole batch.

The heads should only represent about .005 percent of your mash. So if you were cooking one gallon of mash, you would toss out the first ounce! Is that so much to sacrifice for good health and great-tasting spirits? I think not!

But just to be safe, let's all just make sure that we stick to fruits, sugars, and grains, and maybe some spuds for the mash. Just nothing that has any real fiber to it or looks in the least bit wood-like, such as seeds? OK? Moving on!

And lastly the tails. As I've noted, this is when you get to the end of your run. With the temperature going up on your still to around 200°F, this is pretty much where you want to back things down and stop your run. Again, one easy way to tell if you are into your tails is to dip your fingers into the output. Another is to look for the multicolored surface in your collector. You can also smell them, and learn that smell. After a few runs, you will easily notice that smell and know that the end has come. Remember, don't be greedy. One gallon of wash at

10 percent should net you about a quart of booze. Or 1.33 bottles (one bottle being a fifth). You can afford to leave a little bit in your pot. Besides, you want this, it's your sour mash for your next run.

At this point you are thinking, OK, I'm good to go, right? Wrong. We still have to make the mash! While running a still gets all the glory, the magic is in the mash!

Recipes

The Whiskeys—These are the most traditional of American spirits. And if you are an American and not wearing a funny-colored skirt and speaking with a brogue, then there most certainly is an *e* in *whiskey*. Whiskey is part of our heritage, our traditions, and even one of the cornerstones of our country's early economy. At its simplest, whiskey is just grain, water, and yeast. From there, though, only the imagination can limit you. In the United States, we recognize half a dozen or so different types of whiskey:

- bourbon whiskey—mash contains 51 percent or more corn
- corn whiskey—mash contains 80 percent or more corn
- rye whiskey—mash contains 51 percent or more rye
- rye malt whiskey—mash contains 51 percent or more malted rye
- malt whiskey—mash contains 51 percent or more Barley
- wheat whiskey—mash contains 51 percent or more wheat.

The rest of the ingredients can be made up from whatever the distiller wants, but usually it's other, similar grains. To be honest some of these whiskeys are more remnants of the past. Malt whiskey or Scotch and bourbon are fairly common, but good luck trying to find a malted rye whiskey, much less a wheat whiskey, at your local supermarket. Sadly, rye is not far behind them on its way out. As such I'm only going to cover the more popular styles in this guide. Maybe I might do a more advanced version down the road and include some of the less well-known drinks.

Also note that all the whiskeys that I will be discussing are straight whiskeys, which means that no additives, such as colors or flavors, are added after the mash is created.

Moonshine—Mountain dew, white lighting, or better known as plain old corn whiskey, this is what all moonshiners fall back on, the reason being that this is the simplest grain alcohol that any fool can make. Typical moonshine is made from 80 percent or more malted corn grain. (Malted, as noted, means that it got wet and has just started to go to seed.) The remaining percentage is usually split between barley and/or rye. But those cooking it on the cheap often substitute a good bit of corn for sugar. Moonshine is so well-known that almost everyone can tell you how to figure out if you got a good batch: the proverbial blue-flame test! Take one teaspoon of shine and put a flame to it. If it burns with an even, consistent, blue flame, it's good to drink. If it is yellow or sputters, it's bad and you need to run it through the still again.

Ok, sanity check time. Distilling is really the second step in making booze, brewing is the first. Brewing is where the alcohol is made and it is an art form by it's self. In this book we don't really have the time to cover everything you need to master brewing AND distilling so we are going to take bit of a shortcut. In a little bit we are going to walk you though your first batch. We are going to make a rum as it is by far the simplest mash to make and it's an excellent neutral spirit that can be used as a base for several different types of drinks.

I still want to give you an idea of what each type of liquor is made from, so I have included a form of a recipe that brewers call a "Grain Bill". This will give experienced brewers most of the information needed to make these spirits. If you are not experienced with brewing then please stick to the rum recipe for now. I have two other books, How to Make Beer! and How to Make Beer Part II – All Grain Brewing, please refer to those books to learn the basics of brewing as well as some advanced techniques. (If you are confused by the beer part don't be, remember that the wash or mash is also called "Distiller's Beer". It's all the same process)

Please note that these bills are based on 1 gallon batches so multiply as needed.

Blue Moon Shine
- One gallon water
- 2 pounds of corn, cracked
- 3 pound of white sugar
- 1 cup of honey

Depending on how warm it is where you keep your mash, it will be ready in three to five days. Just make sure to follow the previously mentioned guidelines in regard to temperature.

Bourbon—Many stories expound on how Kentucky bourbon got its name. I prefer the one from Stefan Gabányi's must-read book *Whisk(e)y*, wherein he tells a tale of moving county lines and ports of departure that in the end show that bourbon was more a general sign of quality than a specific point of origin. Regardless, today to be legally called bourbon a whiskey must be made in the United States, be 51 percent corn mash, be aged in new charred-oak barrels, be distilled to be no more than 160 proof, and be bottled at 80 proof or higher. To be "straight" bourbon, it must have no additives and be aged for at least two years.

A bourbon mash is usually between 51 and 80 percent corn grains, but a higher percentage makes a sweeter mash; 75 to 78 percent is common, combined with 5 to 15 percent malted barley or brewer's malt and 5 to 15 percent rye, sometimes replaced with wheat for a milder mash. The distillate must not exceed 80 percent ABV, the reason being that a higher percentage would lead to less taste in the product, although distillers usually do not come close to 80 percent. The practical limit is nearer to 70 percent. Most distillers are in the range of 55 to 65 percent. Wild Turkey (forget what non–bourbon drinkers think; of the entire mass-market large-batch bourbons, this is the best) distills out at around 55 percent. The lower proof of distillation produces a heavier, heartier flavor with more grain characteristics. Distillers who want lighter whiskey distill out at the high end and then dilute the distillate with water before barreling. Either way, whiskey usually goes into a new, charred-oak barrel at between 65 and 70 percent ABV. Just to compare, Jim Beam (the Pepsi of bourbons) is barreled around 80 percent ABV, while Wild Turkey is barreled at around 55 percent. Since Jim Beam is sold at 80 proof, its distillers take the aged bourbon and then cut it 50 percent with distilled water. Wild Turkey is bottled at 101 proof. This means that Wild Turkey must distill almost twice as much as Jim Beam to bottle the same amount. See what I mean? This is why Wild Turkey has a richer, fuller flavor.

For real bourbon the distillate must be aged in a barrel made of charred American white oak for a period of not less than two years. Most are aged five to eight years. Aging longer than nine or ten years is not usually done.

Pro Tip—I take white oak and cut into one-inch-square cubes and then char them. I then place the cubes in large-mouthed glass jars or jugs along with the whiskey, and put the lids on. Leave a tiny, pinprick-size breathing hole for the bourbon. I let this set for four weeks, sloshing the jars every time I walk past it. This will "age" your bourbon one year for every month. I came up with this technique years ago. I now hear that several wineries in California are using this same technique to age their wines. Coincidence? I think not!

King's Creek Bourbon
- 1 gallon strained and purified creek water
- 1 pound corn, cracked
- ½ pound wheat grain
- ¼ pound rye
- 1 pound of dry malt extract
- After distilling, age in white oak charcoal chips

Pro Tip—Don't take my word as gospel on this, but I've been told by men older and wiser than me that you can't really use too much yeast, reasonably speaking that is. Don't go full speed stupid and make a batch that's 50 percent yeast. It will probably become sentient and try to take over. But seriously, err on the heavy side. Too much won't hurt you, but too little could mean not enough alcohol production.

Rye—This type of whiskey was very popular prior to Prohibition. It is pretty much the opposite of bourbon.

Rye Neck Whiskey
- 1 gallon purified water
- 1 pound rye
- ½ pound wheat grain
- ¼ pound corn, cracked
- 1 pound of dry malt extract
- After distilling, age in white oak charcoal chips

Tennessee — An official whiskey since 1941 and now legally defined by NAFTA. The law recognizes "a straight Bourbon Whiskey authorized to be produced only in the State of Tennessee." Distillers in Tennessee lobbied for this ruling so as to officially brand their product both in the United States and overseas. While it does qualify as bourbon, most distillers do not use that label in an effort to further distinguish themselves. What really sets it apart is the "Lincoln County" process. This is a filtering process where the whiskey is passed through ten to twenty-two feet of charcoal made from sweet maple. It is then aged for around two years in oak barrels. This forced filtration process helps speed up the polishing of the liquor. The recipe for this is the same as for bourbon. Just make a filter of sweet or sugar maple charcoal chips and then age in charred oak.

Scotch Whiskey—Or just Scotch. There are six regions or types of Scotch; these are based on taste as well as geographical location: Lowlands, Highlands, Speyside, Campbeltown, Islay, and Islands. Scotches are then divided into five categories: single malt, single grain, blended malt, blended grain, and, yep, you guessed it, blended.

Pro Tip—Single? Blended? What does this all mean? Much as a lot of winemakers today blend varietals, whiskey makers will take several different runs from different distillers and mix them together to come up with the taste that they are looking for. On the other end of that spectrum are people who are trying to come up with a very unique flavor and in doing so stick with only one type of ingredient, thus a single malt or a single grain. This is not to be confused with the term single barrel. Normally a distiller will take a bunch of barrels from the aging house and then mix them together with a back set. Distillers do this for continuity of flavor. That way if you buy a bottle today, it will pretty much taste like a bottle you buy five years from now. The other end of the spectrum from this is single barrel whiskey. This means that the distiller took one barrel, cracked it open, and bottled it with nothing else except some water to dilute it to the proper proof. Some people prefer this as it tends to be more distinctive in flavor. But now back to Scotch.

From Wikipedia—The Scotch Whisky Regulations 2009 define "Scotch whisky" in UK law. Under the legislation, Scotch whisky has been

- produced at a distillery in Scotland from water and malted barley (to which only whole grains of other cereals may be added);
- processed at that distillery into a mash;
- converted at that distillery to a fermentable substrate only by endogenous enzyme systems;
- fermented at that distillery only by adding yeast;
- distilled at an alcoholic strength by volume of less than 94.8 percent; and

- wholly matured in an excise warehouse in Scotland in oak casks of a capacity not exceeding seven hundred liters for at least three years.

In addition, "Scotch whisky"

- retains the color, aroma, and taste of the raw materials used in, and the method of, its production and maturation;
- has no added substances, other than water and plain (E150A) caramel coloring; and
- has a minimum alcoholic strength by volume of 40 percent.

Scotch is made in pretty much the same way as bourbon but substituting barley for corn. It gets its distinctive smoky flavor from a process called peating. This is the process of using peat to smoke the malted barley, much in the same manner that you would smoke meat. The smoke from the burning peat infuses the barley, and then that flavor is carried through the fermenting and distilling processes.

To be honest there are as many different ways to make Scotch as there are ways to drink it. It really does deserve a book of it's own. Another project for another time, but until such a time, here is an Upper Lowlands single malt recipe.

Kincaid's Tartan

- One gallon purified Water
- 2 pounds single row barley, malted
- Very lightly smoke the barley with peat and grind to a powder
- Distill and age in oak chips (not charred)
- I do not color mine, but it's up to you

Peat too hard to find? I have heard of people just adding liquid smoke to their mash after fermenting. Not something I have done, but you are welcome to try it and let me know how it works for you. Don't screw it up or you will have to—wait for it—rePEAT the whole process. (I'm a bad man who has a weakness for bad puns, deal with it.)

Irish Whiskey—Whiskey made in Ireland is usually distilled three times. No thumper is used. Irish distillers commonly produce single malts like Bushmills 10 Year and older, single grains like Greenore 8 Year and older, or blends like Jameson and others. Irish whiskey is also usually made without peat in a column still and as such has a lighter flavor than Scotch.

Dagda's Flask

- 1 gallon purified water
- 1½ pounds single row barley, malted
- ½ pound single row barley, unmalted
- Distill 3 times for higher purity
- Age in oak chips (not charred)

Canadian Whiskey—By Canadian law, for a whiskey to be called Canadian it must be produced and aged in Canada. It must be distilled from a mash made of cereal grains and then it must be aged in, "small," wood barrels for three years or more. And get this; it must "possess the aroma, taste and character generally attributed to Canadian Whiskey." Talk about some vague regulations.

In fact I often feel that Canadian whiskey is whatever you care to call it. Most brands are blended whiskeys. They are allowed to add caramel color AND flavorings. It can be distilled at very high ABV levels. And Canadian law makes no distinction between rye and regular whiskey. In fact many of the whiskeys sold in Canada as "rye" whiskey actually contain more corn than rye. I will not offer up a recipe as such, so feel free to put whatever you like in the pot and call it Canadian whiskey. Moving on.

Vodka—A clear, strong liquor with little smell or other strong tastes like you would find in a whiskey. Vodka is made from grains, potatoes, and even fruits. It is widely believed that vodka was first made in Russia in the eighth or ninth century, and many feel that the Russians still make the best. However, as time went on the process of distilling in Russia was slow to change and adapt to new and better techniques. This was due to various economic reasons. As such, many of the traditional Russian vodkas are more flavorful and unsuited to Western palates that feel the best vodkas are tasteless. Regardless of where it comes from, vodka is always distilled to a high potency, 80 to 90 percent ABV, in a column or fractional still. It is then cut with clean, often distilled water, usually to 40 percent ABV, or 80 proof.

The manufacture of vodka can be a very scientific process but I'm going to give you three very typical old-world recipes.

Swedish—Blonde

- 1 gallon distilled water
- 1 pound wheat
- ½ pound rye
- ½ pound sugar
- 1 pound of dry malt extract
- Use a fractional or column still for best results
- Triple filter through activated carbon

Finnish—Dancing Reindeer

- 1 gallon distilled water
- 1½ pounds rye
- ½ pound oats
- ½ pound honey
- 1 pound of dry malt extract
- Finnish as before, and no that isn't a typo

Finnish-style vodkas are also referred to as Polish-style.

Russian—Baba Yaga's Elixir of Youth

- 1 gallon distilled water
- 1½ pounds wheat
- ½ pound potatoes
- ½ pound beets
- 1 pound of dry malt extract
- Finish as before

While most Western drinkers of vodka feel that good vodka is dry and odorless, real traditional Eastern vodkas will have quite a bit of character.

Californian—PRC Approved (NEW)

- 1 gallon distilled water
- 2 pounds mature white grapes, or better yet, "frost grapes" (crushed)
- Finish as before

Pro Tip—A new trend in vodka is flavored, or infused, vodkas. Infusing your vodka with flavor is very easy. Just use a good-size glass jar with a top. Cut up your fruit or whatever your ingredient is and place in the bottom of the jar; the more the better. Fill with vodka till it covers everything. Close lid and place in back of refrigerator or other dark, cold place. Do not freeze. While it's true that the vodka will not freeze, your ingredients probably will and as such you won't get much transfer of flavor. Wait about a month or to taste. Strain and serve.

Gin—The drink that is synonymous with all that it means to be British: dry, cold, and a little bitter. Gin is a very neutral alcohol much like vodka, and if it wasn't for one small twist the two would be indistinguishable: that twist, though, is where magic happens.

Mumbai Ruby

- 1 gallon distilled water
- 1 pound corn, cracked
- 1 pound rye
- 1 pound of dry malt extract

Now as far as distilling you have two options. Either distill once through a column still with a modified slobber box or through a pot still with modified thumper. In the slobber box, the input pipe should be lower so that the vapors can then rise back up through a basket or mesh containing various botanicals (see figure 8); it is in essence a filter. In this basket you will place black peppercorns, crushed almonds, lightly zested lemon peels, liquorices, orris root, chopped lemon grass, angelica, coriander, cassia, cubeb, grains of paradise, and a whole lot of juniper berries—at least 50 percent of your mix.

#8 - Gin Thumper

As the steam passes through the thumper, it will pick up the flavor of the juniper berries and other ingredients, and the end result will be a nice, full-bodied gin.

Rum—The drink of pirates and witch doctors. The drink of the islands! Rum is probably the simplest of all alcohols to make. Sugar, water, yeast, and that's pretty much it. Now how you get that sugar will affect the taste, but it can be as simple or as complex as you care to make it. To me rum will always be something I associate with the Caribbean. For a long time in the United States, if your drink of choice was rum you had very few choices, Bacardi or Meyers, and that was about it. For most people rum was either something you put in a Coke or something floated on top of another drink and then lit on fire. But finally the rest of the world opened it eyes to what the islanders have known for a long time. There is such a thing as good rum, a drink that should be sipped straight and savored; right along a single malt Scotch or a Kentucky bourbon, good rum is a treasure indeed.

Rum from the islands is traditionally made from sugarcane or sugarcane juice, but in truth it can be made from any sugar-based product: molasses, beets, and even grapes. Traditional styles of rum include

- silver rum, very light neutral spirit usually used in mixed drinks;
- gold rum, a more flavorful rum used in "premium" mixed drinks;
- dark rum, very flavorful and either consumed straight or in a drink;
- high-proof rum, either lit on fire or used to add a punch to other drinks;

- spiced rum, infused with the flavors from the Spice Islands; and
- flavored rum, infused with fruits and such, much as vodkas are flavored.

After distilling, rum is aged in oak casks, if not used bourbon barrels. The color of the rum is determined by the type of barrel it is aged in and how long it ages.

Red Beard's
- 1 gallon distilled water
- Heat to boiling, then turn off burner
- 3 pounds brown sugar
- Stir till thoroughly dissolved
- Remove from heat and allow to cool to 70°F
- Pour into fermenter
- Pitch yeast and seal the fermenter
- Add your air lock and store in an appropriate place
- After distilling, age in charcoal chips that were previously used for bourbon

To make a spiced rum or flavored rum, simply use the same process as used in vodka. If you are using bananas, I recommend a good ripe yellow banana. Under-ripe bananas will pass along that green taste from the banana, while overripe bananas will fall apart, become mush, and be a pain to strain out. Fresh caramel is also often used to flavor and color rum.

For Red Beard's Spicy Wench, infuse a bottle of rum with a cinnamon stick, a small piece of star of anise, a clove, a small piece of allspice, a small piece of nutmeg, and a piece of orange zest. Mix in fresh caramel to taste.

Mescal/Tequila—Mescal is the traditional Mexican liquor. It can be hard to get good ingredients, and the process for making good mescal can take a long time, but the end result is something truly remarkable. For those who don't know, tequila is a mescal but not all mescals are tequila. The difference is that tequila is only made from the blue agave plant, as opposed to just any old agave.

Baja Jack's
- 1 gallon distilled water
- 1 pound sugar
- 32 ounces 100 percent pure blue agave extract
- After distilling, age in white oak chips (not charred)

Pro Tip—Worms are not a traditional part of mescal or tequila! It was a marketing gimmick that seems to have paid off. Don't do the worm.

Remember, these are just some of the more basic recipes—you know, just to get your feet wet. I'll be back in another volume where we will tackle each family of liquors with a little more gusto and explore some of the more advanced distillation techniques. But don't worry about that for now. Focus on the basics.

Remember, when the man was asked, "How do you get to Carnegie Hall," he responded with "Practice, practice, practice!"

Making Your First Batch

This is Moonshine 101. Let's get ready to make your first batch. We will start with the easiest recipes:

White Sugar Rum

Items you will need:

- Large stockpot
- Large spoon
- Fermenting jug, bucket, or suitable container.
- Vapor lock and stopper
- Thermometers
- And of course your still – I suggest starting out with the teapot still but the choice is yours.

Ingredients

- 1 gallon of water
- 3 pounds of sugar. White will work but brown sugar will work better.
- Yeast. I recommend turbo yeast, but any yeast will do. You could even get away with using baker's yeast but I'd use a starter for that.

Before you do anything else, STERILIZE EVERTHING.

Ok, bring the water in your pot to a hard boil and then turn off the heat. Slowly pour in your sugar while stirring. Continue to stir until all of the sugar has been completely dissolved into the water.

Now take your pot and put the whole thing into an ice bath either in a larger bucket or maybe the sink. Allow it to cool down to about 70°F. Add ice to the bath as needed. DO NOT add any ice or anything else to the wash as it will contaminate it.

Once the wash has reached the proper temperature you can pour it into a clean fermenting container. Now pitch your yeast into the fermenter, seal it all up and shake! Then add the vapor lock and place in a dark room with consistent temps in the 70°F to 75°F range.

Check it every day, and after three to five days in warm weather and up to two weeks in cold weather (55°F to 60°F) you should be ready. You will be able to tell when it's finished by the lack of activity in the airlock. Also if you have a hydrometer it should read as if there is no sugar in it.

Depending on how good a job you did, your mash will be between 5 and 12 percent ABV unless you used high-strain yeast, in that case it could be almost 20 percent.

Distilling—Take your mash and fill your still two-thirds full. Seal it up and turn up the heat, but when the temperature reaches 160°F start cooling your condenser. Try to keep the temperature between 173°F and 200°F. The object of distilling is to boil off the alcohol and leave the water in the kettle. Alcohol boils at 173°F and water at 212°F. Also remember to take your temps from the top of the head of the still if you can.

Pro Tip—Remember to have good ventilation and keep everything away from any open flames!

Go slow, speed kills! Well, at least it will ruin your batch, and we don't want that. For this first run, don't worry about making any cuts. Since with a pot still you almost always run your distillate twice, it's easier to do the cuts on the second run, as your foreshots and tails will be more concentrated.

On the first run, the strength of your product should be about 18 percent ABV if you started with grains and about 25 percent if you started with fruits. On the second pass, this jumps to 58 to 85 percent for grain, and 60 to 85 percent for fruits.

Periodically taste your output to make sure it still has a strong alcohol taste. When it starts to get a little watery, it's almost time to stop. Let it go a little past here and then cut the heat.

On future runs you may want to separate your cuts on the first run for blending later, but for this one we are just going to keep the whole run as a single batch.

OK, clean out your still and prepare for run number two!

Same thing this time, except throw out the foreshots. I like to collect my output in many small containers. That way I can easily monitor my output and separate the different qualities. Keep tasting your output. Once it starts to get watery, make a cut. Keep running past this point. You are going to save this cut and add it to your next batch. This is called a back set.

That's it! You have now done what everyone said you were crazy for even thinking of trying! Age or polish to taste and enjoy!

Advanced Tips

Salt—Some people add salt to their wash. It will help to increase the boiling temperature of the water and will not carry over while being distilled. Always use non-iodized salt.

Boiling Chips—You might want to consider throwing a couple of boiling stones, or chips, in your pot. When a liquid reaches its boiling point it will need to form bubbles. These bubbles form anywhere there are irregularities in your pot. But if your pot is too smooth there won't be any places for these bubbles to form. Your mash could get superheated and could even explode. Boiling chips prevent this. These are any rough-surfaced, inert object, such as bits of glass, ceramic, or even a couple of marbles. The rough surface provides a site for bubbles to start to form and prevent any superheated vapor explosions.

Blending—The process of mixing different types of liquor to make the taste you desire is often done not just with whiskey but also with rum to achieve just the right quality of light, dark, or black rum. Sherry is sometimes added to certain Scotches.

Charcoal and Wood Flavoring—It is estimated that around 80 percent of the flavor of bourbon and whiskey comes from the oak barrels in which these liquors are stored. We can replicate those flavors by soaking our spirits with oak chips or shavings. Start by using ten (one-inch-square) charcoal pieces per gallon of alcohol, and let it soak for a week. Taste test frequently to find the level of flavor intensity that suits you—whether a little more oak, or longer aging, or a different percentage of alcohol, or different levels of oak toasting.

Oaking—Several different flavors can come from a single type of oak if alcohol strength is adjusted during maturation: 51 to 55 percent ABV will give vanillas, 45 to 50 percent will give a mix of vanillas and sugars, and 40 to 44 percent will give sugars.

To make your own charcoal, wrap oak chips/shavings in aluminum foil and roast them on the bbq. The temperature that you toast the oak at will affect the flavors that are released by the charcoal. A lower temperature will give you a simple oak flavor, as you increase the temperature you will get sweet, vanilla, toast, or even almond flavors. Do not go past 500°F.

Pro Tip—For those of you in wine country, try calling a couple of local wineries and see what they do with their old barrels.

The Hangover—Hangovers are mostly caused by dehydration. Drink lots of water, and I mean a lot, BEFORE you start drinking. The next morning do not eat, just keep drinking that water and take some Advil. Whatever you do, do not fall for the "hair of the dog" bit. That will just add insult to injury.

Final Words

Distilling is done at a junction where science and art meet. To be decent at this, you need only master one side of the equation, but if you ever want to be the best, you have to find a way to join both science and art together. I hope you have enjoyed reading this book as much as I enjoyed all the work and taste tests that went into making it. Also remember that for now, at least in the United States and most other countries, it is illegal to do anything in this book without a license. And that license is pretty much impossible to get without about fifty thousand dollars in your back pocket.

There is no reason for there not to be an exemption for small-batch home distilling just like we have for wine and beer. Heck, in many states you can grow marijuana in your backyard but not brew up a kettle of whiskey. And if you say it's medical marijuana, I will just refer you to the main ingredient in most cough syrups. If they argue "public safety," tell them to check out "Turkey Frying Fire" on YouTube. And if you think that's unsafe, check out the mortality rates for Chicken Carbonara or home gardening for that matter.

The fact is that the government should answer to the people and not the other way around. I wrote this book to educate people on how damned stupid simple home distilling is and to show them that all the horror stories that they have heard about moonshiners are, for the most part, simply not true. So please take a few minutes and send an e-mail to your congressperson and your senator and tell them that we want the Home Distiller's Exemption Bill ASAP or perhaps they should start looking for a new job.

Thank you all, and keep an eye out for our upcoming extended volumes about stuff like grappa, liqueurs, and schnapps, brandy, and cognacs. And advanced books on whiskeys, vodkas, rums, and tequilas. Don't worry, there is more in store!

Welcome to the other side.

Jeff King
HPC (Head Pirate in Charge!)

www.LegalizeMoonshineNow.com

Questions, Comments, and Thanks

Be sure to visit our website at www.TheHomeDistiller.com, or you can also find us on Facebook at http://www.facebook.com/TheHomeDistiller.

There you can post questions and comments, find links to materials and tools, access videos and advanced techniques as well as an FAQ section. See you there!

For supplies please check out our Amazon store at www.MoonshiningSupplies.com

For non-technical questions or general information please send e-mails to help@thehomedistiller.com.

Special thanks to Lavender Simone, our cover girl. If you would like to submit your picture to be a Moonshine Girl please send an e-mail to girls@thehomedistiller.com.

Extra thanks to Max Johnson, illustrator and photographer extraordinaire. It's with his help that *The Home Distiller's Workbook* has gone from simple scribble to the glamorous multimedia experience it is today!

Special Thanks: This goes out to my home team. To my beautiful wife, Jesse, and my three children:

- Duncan, my Big Bear!
- Eleanor, a.k.a. Little Miss Princess
- And our tiniest goblin, Griffin

You are my greatest adventure!

FOI Publishing

FOI Publishing is wholly owned by me and my family. It is the umbrella under which I self publish all my titles. I am a huge proponent of self publishing and should you have any interest in writing a book please feel free to contact me, I'm always willing to try and help others find the success I've had.

My other books:

- How to Make Beer: The Home Distiller's Brewbook
- How to Make Beer Part II: All Grain Brewing Techniques
- How to Build a Still: The Home Distiller's guide to Stills
- Red, White & Blush: A simple guide to the world of Wine

www.FOIPub.com